D0878315

PROOF

Karina Borowicz

Codhill Press
New Paltz, New York

CODHILL

Codhill books are published by David Appelbaum for Codhill Press

Grateful acknowledgments are due to the editors of the following
publications where some of these poems first appeared:

AGNI: "Dog Adrift: Poland, January 2010," "My People";
anderbo.com: "Bad Honey"; *Arts & Letters*: "Snake"; *Barnstorm*: "Guardian";
Barnwood: "Paintbrush"; *The Café Review*: "Window Watching at Midnight";
Columbia Poetry Review: "In Memory," "Marina Tsvetaeva Home Museum";
Connotation Press: An Online Artifact: "Planet Kepler 22B," "Sunbeam Bread";
Contrary: "Carving," "Tools"; *Crab Creek Review*: "Émigré"; *DMQ Review*:
"The Invisible"; *Etchings*: "Perseids"; *The Evansville Review*: "Statue"; *Faultline*:
"Swimming Out"; *Fourteen Hills*: "The Hailstones Bit"; *The Fourth River*:
"Blue Heart"; *Hanging Loose*: "Armadillo," "Cuckoo Clock"; *Harpur Palate*:
"Sanctuary"; *Hunger Mountain*: "Charo," "Tiny Tim"; *Make: A Chicago
Literary Magazine*: "Folk"; *The Midwest Quarterly*: "Idea of Poppies";
MiPOesias: "Iggy Pop on *The Dinah Shore Show*," "My Salt,"
"The Horse's Neck"; *New Ohio Review*: "Midnight Train"; *Nimrod
International Journal*: "Edges"; *Poet Lore*: "Saw"; *Poetry Northwest*:
"Frozen Boot"; *Qarrtsiluni*: "Fist," "Rubber"; *REAL: Regarding Arts and
Letters*: "Bookshop *Biblio Globus*," "Reading *Madame Bovary*"; *RHINO*:
"Fourth of July"; *Ruminate Magazine*: "Down Here"; *The Southern Review*:
"Miniature," "Moose," "Proof," "Reading *Anna Karenina*,"
"Rose Marie on *The Dick Van Dyke Show*"; *The Sow's Ear Poetry Review*:
"Blake"; *Upstreet*: "Emily's Dress"; *Valparaiso Review*: "Genie the Imprisoned Child";
Water~Stone Review: "Bone Flute," "Brush and Ink Herd of Horses"

Book and cover design by Alicia Fox
www.aliciafoxdesign.com

Library of Congress Cataloging-in-Publication Data
Borowicz, Karina.
[Poems. Selections]
Proof / Karina Borowicz. — First Edition.
p.   cm
Includes bibliographical references and index.
ISBN 1-930337-75-2 (alk. paper)
I. Title.

PS3602.O767A6 2014
811'.6—dc23

2014011965

For Ben and Milda

CONTENTS

I

II

III

PROOF

I

The Invisible

Their howls and yips travel the half-mile
over the black field and into the house.
The invisible is calling. Those wild lives

so seldom considered are carrying on
without us, who like to believe that our eyes
have grasped it all. But what about

the matted fur, the bared teeth?
What about the chase that has already begun?
The deer slipping between trees

in the moonless woods. That darkness.
Who among us has seen even a common thing,
an owl, with our own eyes?

Planet Kepler 22B

They say they've found another
earth out there, greening like the shaded side
of a boulder.

I don't know which direction
of the night sky to face.
But that planet's there somewhere,
anywhere, despite me.

Despite everything that's turning here
with me. The sleeping
winter colony of ants,

the radio tower's red star
spilling the light of invisible mandolins,

the inner earth, our real
Milky Way, that glitters
with the minerals of ancestors,

the cave walls at Lascaux, where a herd
of red horses still circles in the darkness.

Brush and Ink Herd of Horses

Here is a man who has run
his hand along the neck of a horse
watched the streaming mane
gallop away

learned a poem of hoof beats
copied it down in bold
fluid strokes
on the unrolled sheet of rice paper

and with the horses he suffers
as his brush moves

the bit burning his mouth
the slicing whip against his thigh
the nails pounding
up through his bare feet

this is how he comes to love freedom

can you forgive my man's heart he cries
as he drives the horsehair brush
filled with ink
over the blinding tundra of paper

Emily's Dress

At the Dickinson Homestead

A replica, no body
ever moved in this
closed a bone button over a wrist

made the thousand ungrand gestures
of a life's unfolding

where is that something real
to lift by the shoulders
and fold again carefully
fabric dingy with a body's passage

seams still tight
with hand-stitched dashes

Window Watching at Midnight

Again the circle of green light.
My neighbor is sewing. With the two
natures of a moth, his hands
hover there, one futility
the other wing hope. And the fabric
is bunched up, from here
it's not clear what until a shirt
dangles its arm.
      Other nights it's something
else, a square of cloth, a sock.
The work smaller and smaller till it appears
nothing's there, but the needle still moves
or what might be a needle, and what might
be thread is pulled, up and out.

Carving

He comes to understand
the spirit abiding in each scrap of wood
that passes through his hands.

Every child is born he says
knowing the language of trees—
for so long our unformed ear
is pressed to the wall of eternity.

With his hands he smoothes the wood
from which a face is beginning
to emerge.

Tools rest at his feet—
the blackened little knife,
a bent nail.

Tools

imagery brings inanimate to life

Hammer and hacksaw, vise and screwdriver have the hard gaze
and slow heartbeat of reptiles. I am visiting the hardware store

with my father. In a wooden drawer stained by dirty fingers
a sea of nails rolls back and forth. The bare light bulb

burning in the middle of the ceiling cuts deep shadows
in the men's faces, silent men that smell of sawdust and kerosene,

boiled cabbage and cigarettes. When I furtively pick up a crested little tool
its claws bite my palm. The neighborhood's only color TV glows neon

in the dark room behind the register. Cowboys are fighting at the bar,
chairs are crashing, the soundtrack builds ominously.

Saw

A boy is learning to cut wood—
in the sun the saw's shadow is the jaw
of an animal tearing the pine plank—
sawdust collects in the creases
of his untied shoes.
When he stops for a moment to size up
the line he's pulling through the soft
white wood
on the other side of the trees
a dog strains against its chain
and cries out.

Cuckoo Clock

The air is thick with minutes.
With years. Barehanded
we can't catch them, so we've armed ourselves
with clocks.

When my father opens
the hut-shaped box, the stream of time
freezes. He oils the gears
and sets the pendulum swinging.
Ghosts swim again like fishes.

It may announce the hour,
but there's so much more
that little bird's hiding.

I saw a hawk this morning
chased by crows,
something squirming in its grasp.

Rubber

Passing the tire factory on the way
to school I'd move through pockets of haunted air,
the sudden warmth of unseen hands would part
across my face, wrist bones of smoke twisting
away. This is my fate, I'd think, only half
hating it, how my life was caught up
in machinery I'd heard yet never seen,
that constant comforting whir behind
painted-over windows. Across the street
in class I'd read about the honey-cured
flesh of pharaohs, the green glow that spilled
from the lab of Madame Curie, but still
nothing changed, even Giza and Paris
reeked with fumes of burning rubber.

Midnight Train

I don't recall ever asking for any of this:
being born, having to live an upstanding
American life, all of a sudden getting old,
coming to fear the very oblivion I would have
preferred in the first place. As a child, I was carried
by a beast of sadness, at the least likely moments
I'd feel it bristle my skin, for instance eating pizza
at the mall, and the feeling would take my breath away.
My greasy fingers had become suddenly so small
and strange, Gladys Knight and the Pips lit the jukebox
with "Midnight Train" and I was dying of this
painful humanness, yet dreading the white noise of heaven.

Passage

When dusk comes a train passes
through the thin woods behind
the cluster of houses

sometimes she's mid-word sometimes reaching
for a coffee cup

when like thunder the crushing machinery
of distance rolls close

and is gone with urgency
an echo trapped
in the stripped branches

a scrap of paper taken by the wind

a voice
she once knew and now
ringing silence

Genie the Imprisoned Child

There's no such thing as silence

she hears the rain, she hears
cars on the street, children
called home by names that sound
like music
there are no words
because no one has ever spoken to her

every day when the patch of sky
she can see from her prison the crib
darkens slightly
someone plays softly
a piano she will never see
the sound comes through the locked window
the sound comes close
something like a touch

something
like the blue that flashes by
she does not know is a bird

Down Here

Blue heron flying low at dusk.

A creature that has never once doubted
its feathers. Or the sky, or the blurring
tops of trees.

Above crossed power lines,
past the abandoned train depot.
It cannot see me.

Its business is not down here,
with us, our lamps burning
dull yellow, like pollen-filled honey,
from behind living room windows.

A secret whirs over us,
startling as a second moon.

I keep driving, but feel
suddenly blind, as after gazing
at a bright and naked light.

Bad Honey

It's not painful anymore to listen
to the radiator tell the truth, to the refrigerator
clear its throat and say two honest words, my ears
have been healed of all the maladies they've been
storing up like bad honey, and now my busy hive
is powered purely and shines with a clean blue light
that's visible even from a distance when I lie
in the field at night counting the drops I've managed
to collect: that face, that sigh, that hand
clutching a bag filled with torn bread, it's music
to me now, all the whining of tiny wings
and rubbing of prickly legs

Hunger

The breadcrumbs beneath the young oak
were buried by last night's storm.

Winter takes nothing away.
Winter gives me
your warm body.

Clothed in black
I make my way across the white field.

Animal silence of snow:
the beauty of a crouching wildcat
whose hunger I don't fear.

I toss the bread.
Crows swim through the deep snow.

Each day, the woodpecker's tapping
comes closer.

Sunbeam Bread

How I hated those white gloves, which smelled
of lavender sachet and whose seams
bit my fingers. After mass I'd hold out my hands,
palms up, and beg my mother to pull them off.

Sundays, too, we'd drive down to the bay
and feed the ducks that week's leftover bread.
It was one of my father's favorite things,
to walk softly to the water's edge
and toss handfuls onto the surface.
Like toy sailboats the ducks would glide
leisurely over to claim the floating crusts.

Once I ventured out onto the boulders.
I looked down and could see the ducks' yellow feet
paddling frantically beneath the surface.

The Horse's Neck

I used to fly a plane around the dented
tin globe, I was a paper pilot
fragile over the churning Atlantic—
that was me drawing chalk lines across the sky
sadly and slowly at first, in the knowledge there were
sharks waiting to take my limbs off, then I'd make
wild scribbles till my shoulder ached—
back then I was always escaping the jaws
of death at the last minute, never forgetting
to put a flourish on it, give it a little English
like the time I was swimming and the undertow dragged me
to open sea, I struggled against the huge soft body
of the water, the minions of seaweed,
everything went gray and flat around me
as if the world had collapsed into an old photograph
and when I was far away from the horse's neck of land
I somehow leapt free of the pull like Jonah spit in a bright
arc from the whale's lips, flapped silver in the sun
and backstroked home to the blessed sand—I will never
ever leave you again, my red pebbles, my beached quahogs
my salt of the earth, my blacktop parking lot.

My Salt

Back then I kept salt in a shaker like a pet.
Setting it free every now and then by
unscrewing the lid, I'd sit and watch
thinking how my salt loves me
it never wants to leave and never wants
to be shaken out. My salt was faithful
through the bitterest times, shining
its white purity, dust of the Milky Way
curled up and snoring sweetly in a little bottle
fitted to the palm of my hand.

The Hailstones Bit

The hailstones bit the ripening
tomatoes—like that, like God decided
suddenly to grow teeth, gnaw on
our corner of the world. The screen door
shredded down the center, three ragged stripes.
It could have been the claw of a hungry bear.
I know what you've got in there. It wanted
our peace. I couldn't blink away
the missing girl's face. That morning,
her body had been found in the Connecticut River
after six days, battered.

Edges

Cold and silver now
night has the thinnest
razor's edge to it
no longer the thick fragrant yellow
of wax and honey

and on the blade of morning
the bees are dying off
I see one in its dying
moving slowly as stiffening wax
clinging with its soft might
to a flower's dried center

the bee's furred body
barely distinguishable
from the zinnia's hardened fur
bristling with seed

Idea of Poppies

I still have that packet of seeds
five years later. Back then
I didn't have any ground in which
to plant, but I took the gift anyway
because I knew I'd miss you, I knew
even a spoonful of black dots
hidden in a sealed envelope was better
than a Sahara of nothing. Poppies, at least,
are something, even if it's just
the idea of poppies I've tucked away
like a prayer card. And now that I've got
more dirt than I know what to do with,
I'm afraid to plant those seeds. Afraid
the life in them has diminished, the utter red
that blooms when I remember you will have lost
strength to appear in the world.

II

Perseids

Stars are falling through the galaxy's thin arms
outstretched across the sky.
Loose fur from a comet's wagging tail
prickling with static.

How still the earth is amidst all this motion.
Yet it's flying and spinning
because it too was flung once.

I watch the stars fall, and my blood
ignites as it feels its way through my body.
As if the hum of everything out there suddenly
here, called my name.

I Stood Still

I stood still and the journey
came to find me
no matter that I was unprepared
the journey carried me along on its back
each step it took
echoed up from the earth and settled
in my bones

we have come so far my body
is filled with hoof beats
when we get there
my weapon will become
my offering
this blade of glittering distance

Pebbles

Saying goodbye to a place is never
easy, how does one go about it, no one
to speak to, no words to say just memories
and regrets that will remain unincarnate.

No one to stop you wandering
that city on the last rain-filled day,
skin pained by the raindrops that are more
falling pebbles.

This is the place where and *how many*
times I passed by here and of course the old
handless statue whose cool features
are the exact word for the situation, this constant reaching
with no hope of touch.

Statue

Whenever I pass
I feel it

the magnetic pull
of a stone's hope.

Lips of stone
that own no tongue.

How tenderly
fingers of light
and shadow brush
the chipped cheekbone.

Bone Flute

We find things, change things. A flute
from a bird's hollow bone. Slanted through
braided hair, a long white feather.

How fascinating our early selves, their leavings
in display cases. Our tarnished
Roman coins. The red shards
of our pottery. Our first attempts
at glass, the small perfumeries peeling in layers
of mica. An iron key, like a lost tooth.
The lid that it fit still buried,
locked in the earth.

How many other things a museum can't contain—
not one vivid dream of the Illyrian girl who wore
this bronze spiral bracelet survives. The soft tissue
of a laugh. An intricately woven song, popular
among the women of her village, frayed and lost.

Emptied of the purpose that once breathed
through it, the bone flute
has come to rest here, upon a mound
of black velvet silence.

Paintbrush

I have a paintbrush of living hair that feels
pain against paper, dipped in green and making
a shadow on the sea, dipped in ochre
building light from scratch, building a great
hidden fire that only I know burns—how many
suns can one man have, when I close my eyes
at night I see them, shining day down into my dreams
shedding light on things that were meant only
for black and silence, I can't help it my paintbrush
has claws and its fur keeps growing

Miniature

Hands knotted with sinew
the painter of miniatures
drags black paint with the tip
of a single white cat hair
to give the shah sight
just one eye
for the face in profile
the second eye unseen
but gazing on the other side
of the Samarkand paper
into the grain of the worktable
a vast plain stained with oil
and flicks of paint
where princes
and tigers are born

A Graven Image

New birds are arriving
because it's spring, or the long
shadow before it, and old birds
return to the spring of memory.
Gulls circle there, stroking the swells
with their wings the way hands
smooth billowing silk. Gulls
of childhood, gulls making footprints
on the sand beside me, staring out to sea,
feathers roughed up with distance.

What's the point in writing
on a blank page with black ink?
I want to cut the words in
with a pin or a penknife,
want them to be there yet
not there, a violence apparent
not to the eye but to wondering fingers.

The Grackle's Yellow Eye

The grackle's yellow eye
what world is it watching?
I see spring coming from all directions
falling from the sky
tiny birch petals
hear it moving up from the ground
a long groan even under
the house.

This morning news of the death
of an infamous man
images of young people dancing
in city streets
I watch the grackle with binoculars
its little nervous eyes bright against
the blue-black feathers.
What is this bird's singular story
that began when it gathered strength
enough to pierce the shell?

The birches are softening
under a green haze
there's warmth in the slender trunks
that I touch as I walk
my house back in the distance.
I try to see it as an animal
sees it from the edge of the woods
without memory or hope.

Pity

I poured water into a bowl
and placed it outside. All water
is from the same source. Pity

the birds who can't find
a puddle to drink from these days.
The chipmunks and squirrels. The snake.

I heard a story of men lost in the desert
for weeks. They hunted snakes and drank
the blood. All water is from

the same source, spigot, sea,
or snake, the watery movement
of my hands. The bowl of caught

water, water stopped in its tracks,
water thrashing in an arc around
the bowl's rim and falling back.

Snake

He was waiting by the doorstep.
With a shudder he sucked in
his secret tongue.

What was in his gaze
that drew a thread of wild stillness
up through me?

Mud-colored, all neck,
he had frozen in an open O.
Everything about him was charged

with instinct: the lifted,
diamond head, the tight line
of his closed lips,

the pin-prick nostrils.
I was the first to move,
not used to suspension, not used

to the slow work of that red thread.
In a sudden scrawl he was gone,
a body of poured water flowing

till the dust drank him in.

Fist

The octopus frightened me the first time
I saw it—I didn't believe
something so strange lived even in a place
I couldn't see.

It flew forcefully through the water
a human hand gesturing
with a dancer's confidence and sometimes
the anger of a fist.

I stood before the tank in the darkened room
beads of spotlight scattering
upon the water's surface
the heavier oil of light
plunging down into that square of cold sea.

Swimming Out

It was dusk when you left
your clothes on the sand
clothes you wouldn't need anymore

the time of day when
years before you used to help bring the sheep
home to the barn

those old sheep with swollen knees
who pulled on the sparse grass
in the seaside pasture

remember the wool grease always on your hands
how it blackened every line and crack

Armadillo

Everything has a string attached,
everything's being reeled in, you wake up
one day to find the rope of years
disappearing around a corner, like that,
snap, the sharp tail of an armadillo, the dark
muscle of a snake, and you want all of it
back, all it's been sneaking off with—*how long
have I been asleep?*—don't answer that.

Guardian

A tiny animal kept close to me on a string.
Warm and precious wool, a little black lamb whose face
is a miniature universe. Then the dream
shifts, I'm walking along my childhood beach
and there's a doll's arm in a nest of seaweed,
a leg pokes from the parted mouth of a blue
quahog shell. Keep walking. A doll's red-cheeked
face, golden curls tumbling in the foam
that pumps in and out at the shore like the edge
of a huge heart. But it's not up to me to put
the doll together. It's understood: I'm here to guard
separation, preside over the widening drift.

Dog Adrift: Poland, January 2010

The terror of small dark eyes
that have given up measuring the vast whiteness.
A dog drifts on the Baltic, hunched
on his little floe of ice. Frozen whiskers, tail folded
beneath his body. There is nowhere to go.
Only the sound of silence breaking
on silence.

Night presses its body down upon the ice
tired after the long hunt. Its gleaming fur
smells of distance, of men's fires.
Night's milk is cold.

They try a long-handled net first.
Then bare hands, grabbing at shoulders,
scruff of the neck. The dog has no further
inside himself to shrink. The men's arms
or the ice. Their shouts echo and the world
has edges again.

Frozen Boot

Before anything made sense and I was wandering
in the ancient city of my ancestors where there was always
rain impending and later the threat of snow
I wrapped a scarf around my head and kept on walking
pausing on Žaliasis bridge the menacing bronze figures
scythe-wielding farmer giant factory worker waiting for me on either end
it was a kind of medicine to be suspended for a while a tiny drop of water
trembling over the icy river and when I finally crossed the bridge
I ran my hand along the frozen boot of the factory worker
because how else do you talk to statues, later I visited Mary's shrine
the air sweating ambergris my lungs purged of breathlessness
and idle chatter my trembling stilled and it was bestowed upon me
on my way back a paper snowflake lying on the sidewalk

Proof

For Adele Chudzik

The day they moved your belongings outside
it snowed, the flakes came to rest on your
stained pillow, huge clustered snowflakes
clung to a pile of paperbacks. The lamp,
its pleated shade askew, wasn't made
for that kind of weather.

A life taken down, brick by brick.
The past being carted away proof
you'll never be back.

Boxes and boxes. Your feet, so tiny
the shoes looked like children's. They emptied
dresser drawers into cartons and lined them up,
open to the sky, a pair of spare eyeglasses
upside down and pooling with melted snow,
an address book sprawled open, names of the dead
in your bold hand. A gold lipstick case.
Tangle of lace curtains, antiqued by cigarettes.

The neighbors thought, *So that's how she lived.*

Moose

At the reading you ended
with the poem about coming close
to death the night you hit a moose
the storm of glass
fur and blood
in the middle of the northern white
nowhere

am I alive
you asked again and again
as snow floated down like ash
settling on your shaking hands
refusing to melt

and when a few years later
you decided to truly die
it was your birthday and summer
was coming into its noisy fullness
but still no answer

In Memory

When she was still able she walked
for miles, covering the same ground each time,
staking her territory. The border collie
just ahead of her, two figures slipping
in and out of the sea fog that banked
the roadside most mornings.

I saw her for the last time
in her garden, ripping handfuls of weeds
and cutting back all the spent blooms.
She'd spend hours out there, browned by the sun
but never really warmed by it. Yet this was how
she needed to remember herself, fingers
black with dirt, bare arms plunging to the shoulders
into the phlox and tangled poppies.

Blue Heart

Walking past that much lavender
was a sort of trial, a sort of bliss
I couldn't stop to savor, and the ghost
of lavender hung about me as I kept moving,
an incense bomb with its smokily transparent arm
hard around my shoulders, and I breathed in
the dusk-colored breath, the blue whisper
with the merest edge of blood spice, something beautiful
has exploded from the earth, I knew this
down to the roots of my fingernails,
something beautiful survives in this city, the clock
of its blue heart is ticking, its thousand
tiny seeds numbered among us.

Folk

If you asked me to choose I'd say the Azoreans
not the thin-lipped progeny of the Quaker captains
of industry. That's the rock and the hard place
I grew up against: the São Miguel fisher folk
with their black rosaries and *fado*; the Yankee
owners of the boulder-strewn pastures by the sea,
salt marshes and haunted paddocks (old man Slade
would roam the fields with a darning needle in his pocket,
jabbing wrens' eggs to save, he said, the bluebirds).
Wild lilies grew alongside tumbledown stone walls
for miles to the beach. But in town, almost every backyard
was a shrine to Fatima: three stone children and a lamb
kneeling before Mary, zinnias planted piously around,
geraniums; red was the color, the Azoreans were used to
life on a volcano, the lush growth that comes from ash.
What they didn't get was the Yankee penchant
for solitude and disdain for music, which seemed more like
a disdain for the depths of joy and sorrow. Living up against the sea
like we did how could you not want to describe it?

III

Fourth of July

Fire bloomed in the sky
then vanished like dandelion seed
the hairs on my arms jumped up
with every pounding explosion
it had something to do with America, with Nixon
with Viet Nam, with history
and I was supposed to feel
happy, I was supposed to
feel small

Tiny Tim

There's no good reason why
things worked out this way
but in the end the golden-throated
ukulele has taken flight
seeking the tree of its origin
a long search in northern forests
that walk slowly in moonlight
antlers in a line searching for patches of lichen
pine nuts larvae dreaming beneath bark
don't worry Tim there's nourishment
even in snow

Iggy Pop on *The Dinah Shore Show*

Remember Soupy Sales, how I wanted
a husband like that, pie in our faces every day,
The Jackson Five on *Carol Burnett*
in green and white bellbottomed suits.
Michael knew how to move and if you
watched his feet like I did you saw
duende in those side-zip boots.
When Bill Cosby introduced the Four Tops
"live from the Apollo!" the crowd screamed but they
went wild for the Temptations—
in the duel between the groups I can't say
who won, the lows and highs of the Temps
got the crowd but who can resist the aching
sincerity, the Tops' raspy edge of heartbreak,
the cliffs they'd lead you to and leave
you standing on, the one in dark glasses clutching you
by the edge of your shirt.
                                  And then there's shirtless Iggy
who went over the cliff and put his scars on display
but he looked out from under his long black bangs
like a little boy, nervous when he had to talk to Dinah,
and as he confessed that the incident with the broken
glass tearing up his chest was a penance
for some bad thing he'd done the night before,
he looked down through the smoked-glass coffee table
and you could tell he was sinning
all over again.

Charo

What is it like to be a woman I
wondered and there was the long
fluffy hair and the bangs down
to her eyelashes, the flamenco streaming
like flashing light from all ten fingers no
from all her body that's when I knew
you've got to have a secret, you've got to
master some light but always some darkness
so you can laugh like a girl and then blow
their minds with what you really are.

Rose Marie on *The Dick Van Dyke Show*

Funny, the unique ladyhood of bows tucked
in a teased bob, black boat-neck dress, white gloves
at the ready all while cracking wise as one tough
Irish nun, it isn't work it's a blessing
to pass the day in a midtown highrise holding your own
with the boys, Morey's cello whimpering every now and again
above the imagined traffic, planes from Queens suspended
over the cardboard skyline barely visible behind the half-open blinds,
always leaving but never managing to be, finally, gone.

My People

Only the women on my mother's side
had long hair then, on my father's side they were
city slickers, bobbed and permed, cashmere sweaters,
cocktail hour and Bing Crosby, the other side didn't
mix with their coiled braids and flowered dresses,
my grandmother in her hut with newspapers stacked
to the ceiling, the goat knocking at her door
with his little black horns, my town aunts in sunglasses
shocked to see my mother's mother cooking beets over wood
and eating dandelion greens for supper, but what did I care,
they were all my people, the windblown beauty
of my mother, my father's white cavalry gloves.

Émigré

In his room there was a small
high window, and it gleamed
at night like a dagger.
The moon's weapon, he mused,
a woman who wants me
to keep my distance.
It was true that distance was all
he owned in the world. At times
even the change in his pocket
seemed out of reach.
He spoke English with an accent;
people cupped their hands
behind their ears. Was he whispering,
after all, or standing in his old
town square half a world away?
He tossed coins at the fountain
just to watch them sink.

Guest Room

The wasps go about their business
in the far corner of the room.
They're drawn it seems,
through no power of their own
into a tiny crevice where the ceiling
and walls meet, dark bodies
sucked into a beyond
that I can't cross. Then one
by one they're pushed
out of that space, refreshed
and eager to continue work
in the world. Their segmented
figures make my neck
prickle with fear, a need
to hide, but I'm told
never mind, there's nothing
from me they could
possibly want.

Sanctuary

They hollowed out the lintel above our door and fought there
every morning, dawn came and they had to shudder their wings
wildly against the wall especially having slept flattened into
that small space; I felt clawed awake every day by something big
and terrible, something intending me harm; though I tucked
handwritten poems of Frost and Blake beneath my pillow for sustenance
and a little light, it was such a dark time, the fighting and flying away,
the coming back loudly to roost.

Blake

I'd go to Blake for solace, for
a nightlight, for a vase of tiger lilies.
The moon was always beyond the trees.
The trees were far away, purple shadows
with hooked claws thrown upon the moon.

The moon was there for a reason
that I couldn't manage to guess. A question,
round and white, sometimes with horns,
looked down upon me, watched me
with animal patience and a gentle face.

One night, a voice came through the window.
There were always voices, this one
more like a silver coin warm from someone's hand.
Blake's hand. But the coin wasn't
an answer, and it couldn't purchase one.

Bookshop *Biblio Globus*

I wander in and let my hands rest
on any book any page
birds have their pick of branches
St. Seraphim page 95 feeds the bear
his last remaining bit of bread
the world's hunger has become his own
in a line of crumbs there are secrets
I'm gathering them up

Reading *Kristin Lavransdatter*

The eyes of the forest are upon her
as she walks alone along the shadowed edge.

No truth exists that a pine doesn't know
no impulse in her fingers
bent now with age
that wasn't first sifted
through the roots' fists in the soil.

As a child she watched her father
carve wood held gently in his powerful hands
peel away the outer layers
to reveal the straight white cross
a secret
the crooked tree had been keeping.

Reading *Anna Karenina*

In middle age Tolstoy apprenticed himself
to a bootmaker. He labored at learning
the skills of that trade. Sometimes his fingers
bled onto the leather as he punched the awl
or drew the needle in the outline of a foot.
Blisters, he knew, are holier than ink stains.
The boots were ugly and they pinched,
Sonya complained, and she refused to wear them.
Yet she copied *Karenina* by hand
how many times? It was his words she loved,
how he formed souls out of air. Just breath.
She preferred the page's purity to his
restless hands. If he were a man made only
of words she'd give her whole self to him.

Reading *Madame Bovary*

The drawer of letters. A tinderbox
of locked-up words. And the noise it makes
upon opening—lies and whispers, the hissing
of a cornered snake.

The sun has buckled the attic floorboards,
hardened the black droppings of the mouse
that long ago curled up beneath the desk
and died, by now all bone,
the gleaming chain of its spine laid bare.

Marina Tsvetaeva Home Museum

The midnight blue gabardine dress
the yellowed kid gloves

it doesn't matter that I can't decipher
the handwriting on the notebook pages
displayed like antique jewelry in the glass case

will she be conjured out of thin
ordinary air
a bouquet of paper roses

the sleeves hang empty

what is the proper equation: dress plus pen
plus lorgnette

signature plus gloves plus prayer book

pearls plus hairbrush plus postcard

desk plus photograph plus mirror

School for the Blind

Photo Exhibit at the Central House of Artists, Moscow

A boy, his scalp covered
with white stubble, his face up close,
all sharp bone, all light
and shadow. In the hollows
of his eyes, darkness runs
too deep to give anything back.

Is it right to gaze so freely
at the blind? My shame
and my tenderness are beating
together. I look away,
then step closer.

Back in the street I'm greedy
for faces. Only these carry with them
a different light, not time-stopped.
These mouths move, these eyes
gaze back, these faces
flicker in the human breeze
as we stream over the sidewalk.
The cobalt beginnings of hair barely visible
on a man's shaven chin. An old woman
whose eyebrows have worn down
to puckered skin. Ears, some red,
some folded, or wing-like. Beneath this angry
winter sky, there's nothing as beautiful
as our bare, imperfect faces.

Yet the photograph stays with me
like the tightened, white line
of a scar. A negative after-image
that glows with otherworldly perfection.

Mystics

The iron grate over the window seems
ancient, as if pulled from the ruins.

The hunched old woman is walking
her lame collie. Have I told myself
this story before?

You said mystics wander the city.
But in the forest I saw a man beneath a pine,
his face twisted by truth.

Why are we thrown here with such brutal force?

The sky is always long ago
and years from now.

Reading St. Thérèse of Lisieux

"The Little Flower"

I wept for visions, prayed
for a voice to invade the silence of my cell.
A violet in a hailstorm—I begged
for such violence, to be battered with purity.
A cold flame to burn me from the outside in.
Wound me with Your touch. Because
I can take it, because the blood of a warrior
was poured into a girl's body, because I'm dying
to gallop into battle with a sword raised
in my fist. I'm filled with rage,
now show me how to make it holy.

My Troubles

Maybe I'm just a symbol after all and I bite
my nails for my panic to be symbolized, I touch the prayer card
in my pocket thinking Mary, Mary, such white skin and bright
red lips, and that robe blue as the eternal
sky, the more you think about it the more fearsome
eternity becomes, and I can't look now
because there's a glow on the horizon
behind her, that's where all my troubles await.

Wild Eye

All day the dream will linger
it won't easily be extinguished
by the lightly falling rain
by the milk of the sun

her hands, taking up
the used breakfast dishes
will not easily forget
the horse's sleek warmth
white mottled with charcoal blue

the wild eye
no answers, no questions
just hooves pounding the damp sand
joyously, again and again
ringing out, an axe against wood
against stone
against the whole world

ABOUT THE AUTHOR

 Karina Borowicz's début poetry volume, *The Bees Are Waiting* (2012), was selected by Franz Wright for the Marick Press Poetry Prize and was named a Must-Read by the Massachusetts Center for the Book. Her poems have appeared widely, including in *AGNI*, *Columbia Poetry Review*, *New Ohio Review*, *Nimrod*, *Poet Lore*, *Poetry Northwest*, and *The Southern Review* and have been featured in *Poetry Daily*, *Verse Daily*, and Ted Kooser's *American Life in Poetry* series. She has published translations from the Russian and the French. Trained as an historian, Borowicz also holds an MFA from the University of New Hampshire. She makes her home in the Connecticut River Valley of Western Massachusetts.